KEYS TO PARENTING KIDS WITH OCD

Effective parenting techniques for managing and understanding your kids with ocd

By Willa Wonka

Table of contents

chapter 1

The truth about kids with OCD

Does your kid possess
persistent, unsettling anxieties, trepidations, or worries?
absurd, routine religious practices?
unwanted, uncontrollable thoughts or mental images?
patterns of behavior or habits that disrupt daily life?
a propensity to seek affirmation repeatedly?
a desire to execute actions "exactly right"
issues with persistent tardiness or sluggishness?
persistent inclinations to clean, arrange, or inspect?
urges to collect pointless items?
a propensity to shun particular locations or activities?
OCD is a very serious condition to the people who must live with it every day and to their family members, even though movies and television productions occasionally treat it as a comedy. OCD was always thought to be a rare condition, but scientists now know that millions of individuals worldwide suffer from it.
OCD affects between five and six million Americans, or two percent and three percent of the population.
Only two other family members would be impacted by OCD, which would leave about 21 million Americans affected.
One in 50 people and one in 100 school-aged children suffer from OCD.
Following phobias, drug addiction, and serious depression as the most prevalent mental diagnoses, OCD comes in at number four.
OCD is one of the top 10 causes of impairment in the world, according to a recent study.
OCD's root etiology is unknown. According to research, there is a brain issue. Insufficient levels of serotonin, a brain neurotransmitter, are seen in OCD sufferers.

Typically, OCD runs in families. Thus, it might be genetic. However, it can also happen if there is no family history of OCD. Streptococcal infections can sometimes cause OCD or exacerbate it.

What signs of OCD do children show?

Each youngster may exhibit a unique set of symptoms. The most typical signs are as follows:

intense preoccupation with dirt or pathogens
persistent uncertainties, such as whether the door is locked
conflicting ideas about using violence, causing injury to or killing someone, or harming oneself
Counting, touching, and thinking about numbers and sequences for extended periods
obsession with precision, symmetry, or order
persistent thoughts of engaging in inappropriate or banned behaviors
having doubts about one's religious convictions
a strong desire to remember or be aware of even the smallest details
Too much focus on details

excessive fear of the worst happening aggressive thoughts, desires, or actions

You observe a friend neatly packing away their work tools as you are both working on a project. You can't help but notice that they've arranged all of their pens in their box so that they are facing the same way and are arranged in order of color. They reply, "Oh." That's just me being OCD,

OCD is frequently so much more than the disorder that is frequently associated with neatness and particularity.

OCD can have a particularly negative impact on children. Any period, possibly as early as three years old, can see the start of symptoms.

To ensure that kids and teenagers who are at risk of developing OCD receive the proper care, parents and teachers must be aware of the risk factors.

OCD is treatable when properly managed. Neglecting it could have major consequences for the child's and the family members' quality of life.
HowContinue to Read to Discover
ROLE OF PARENTS IN MANAGING OCD
How to spot signs of OCD in children and teenagers
How to effectively manage and treat OCD in children
OCD: What Is It?
A pattern of unwanted and bothersome thoughts, concerns, pictures, or sensations that cause distress (such as anxiety, disgust, or "not right" sensations) and repetitive behaviors intended to soothe that distress are the hallmarks of obsessive-compulsive disorder.

These undesirable thoughts are frequently referred to as obsessions. Compulsions are unwanted, recurrent habits or mental practices.

Most people occasionally have unwelcome thoughts throughout their lives. These undesirable ideas won't be taken seriously if the person does not have OCD, thus they won't be as distressing. Obsessions and compulsions that have a clinically negative effect on a child's life are the distinguishing features of OCD.

For instance, unpleasant thoughts may be so severe that kids have problems falling asleep at night. The child may have trouble leaving the house to go to school, play sports, or carry out their daily routine because the repetitive behaviors are so upsetting and hindering.

a doctor converses with a young girl
For a child or teen, OCD can be devastating, but with the right psychiatric care, there is hope.

The good news is that OCD has been extensively researched and that there are effective treatments available. Similar to other mental health disorders, this condition can be treated more quickly the earlier it is diagnosed.

It is critical to examine the obsessions and compulsions that underlie OCD in detail to provide children with the care they require.

What Are Obsessions, Exactly?
Concerning OCD, obsessions are fears that kids, teens, and other people can't stop thinking about. OCD sufferers frequently recognize that something is "wrong," and they frequently realize that the thoughts they are having are abnormal.

Despite their best attempts, people appear unable to stop thinking about these things, which might make them anxious.

The following are a few of the most typical types of obsessions:

fear that no matter what they do, they will pass away or become ill
Fear that a loved one will suffer harm, become ill or pass away Worry that they will break a law and receive a harsh punishment for it
Fear of touching things out of concern that they might be dirty
Obsession with making sure that everything is organized, even, and in its proper place
Fear that if something isn't done in a certain order, bad things will happen.

The fact is that everyone occasionally has unwanted thoughts. The distinction between OCD and sporadic unwanted thoughts is that children with OCD can't stop thinking about these thoughts and sometimes become paralyzed by them. These obsessions are frequently so severe that children are unable to think about anything else.

What Are Compulsions, Exactly?

A youngster must experience both obsessions and compulsions to be diagnosed with OCD.

Compulsions are strict and frequently repeating mental or behavioral patterns. These compulsive behaviors, which frequently take the shape of routines, are intended to reduce stress or avert potentially terrifying results.

Children with OCD must repeat these acts in a specific sequence over and over again. If they don't, their obsessions take control and they start to worry that something bad will happen. These actions could be related to symmetry, cleanliness, orderliness, or safety. Children are forced to start over if they aren't done "exactly right."

These actions might be thought of as rituals that provide kids with a source of power. They believe they can influence what happens next by performing these repeating behaviors in a specific way.

The following are some of the most prevalent examples of compulsions:

having to consistently wash or clean items a certain way
Repeating phrases in your head until they "feel correct"
having to repeatedly recreate, edit, or read something after erasing it
To say a word or phrase more times than necessary until it is uttered precisely once or in precisely the proper way
ensuring that every door in the house is locked several times, or repeatedly going in and out of the doors
checking to make sure all of the lights are out before you leave the house
ensuring that each homework assignment was completed correctly by reviewing it a predetermined number of times.
chewing each bite the same amount of times on both sides of the mouth
arranging everything in a predetermined, even, symmetrical arrangement
counting everything and anything too specific lucky numbers to avoid bad numbers
It's crucial to remember that compulsions frequently develop from adaptive habits. Children should, for instance, double-check their homework to make sure it was completed correctly.

On the other hand, this starts to have a clinically negative effect on not just their lives but also the lives of family members if kids wind up checking their homework a dozen times to the disadvantage of other activities.

The same may be said for making sure that doors are closed and that all lights are off. Before departing, it's a good idea to check sure the residence is secure. However, this becomes a significant problem if it stops the family from leaving the house.

Taking Back Her Freedom
Patient and doctor
Learn about the struggle a young patient faced to beat OCD.

Controlling Her OCD
How Can OCD in Children Be Spot?
Recognizing the potential symptoms of OCD in children is crucial for people like parents, teachers, and athletic coaches. The sooner you can step in at the first sign of a mental health issue, the greater the likelihood that the intervention will be beneficial.

There are many typical developmental rituals, such as sleep rituals, that are not related to OCD. But if a ritual starts to interfere with a child's ability to function, that can help determine whether it's more than just a routine and may be an indication of OCD.

OCD frequently grows gradually over time. Due to the gradual onset of symptoms and a parent's innate desire to comfort and protect their child, it may be challenging for adults to recognize a child's OCD symptoms when they first emerge.

It might be simpler to see how OCD affects children's and the people around them's quality of life.

There are several things to look out for that could be OCD symptoms.

Not all of the following symptoms indicate OCD. They are illustrations of actions that might indicate that a young person is in distress and may require assistance from a qualified adult.

Homework
OCD in children can cause them to take too long to finish their assignments. Children may be required to read the same passage repeatedly, write each number exactly as they appear in a math problem, or have their schoolwork checked so many times that it takes a very long time to complete.

Away from the House

When leaving the house, a family with OCD-affected children may take longer.

For instance, if a youngster is spending a long time getting dressed, they may be making sure that every door, window, and light is in the "correct" places or working properly before leaving. They could become upset if they try to leave before the ritual is done.

The family is frequently perpetually late for activities as a result of this tendency.

Handwashing

When it comes to OCD, handwashing is one of the most well-known compulsions.

Handwashing may be motivated by obsessions with germs, feelings of disgust, or other types of contamination, such as "bad emotions," or worries about becoming stressed, anxious, or worried all the time. Look for any evidence of raw, bleeding skin on the hands if handwashing is associated with OCD.

If kids wash their hands frequently during the day, the soap will irritate their skin, causing scarring, skin peeling, and bleeding.

Alcohol or drugs

Children may use drugs as a coping method occasionally when they are having trouble managing a condition. Teens who are struggling with their mental health may feel overwhelmed, misunderstood, or socially isolated. Sometimes, this results in drug abuse.

Sleep Patterns

OCD frequently interferes with getting to sleep or staying asleep. OCD children might need to follow a very specific regimen before going to bed and drifting off to sleep. If individuals experience intrusive thoughts or worries that are more acute at night, they can also have trouble falling asleep. They have to start the process afresh if it is interrupted for any reason.

OCD frequently extends the bedtime routine by 30 minutes, an hour, or even more. Children are deprived of essential sleep, which affects their ability to learn, their emotional growth, and their interactions with peers and family members.

Consistent sleep disruption can also have a detrimental impact on how well CBT and other OCD therapies work.

Don't forget

Not all of the manifestations of OCD in children are represented by these behaviors. Additionally, it does not imply that if a child has problems with them, they have OCD.

These are just a few instances where a young child could have uncomfortable thoughts, feelings, or sensations and then act out or avoid the situation to feel better.

Parents should think to consider talking to a qualified expert about the possibility of OCD if this cycle of discomfort and relief causes family distress or dysfunction.

View Now!

Obsessive-compulsive disorder is highlighted by Dr. Elizabeth McIngvale.

Like other mental health conditions, there is seldom just one cause for a child to acquire OCD.

The following list of risk factors is far from exhaustive, but it does give a brief overview of what might contribute to the emergence of OCD. It is crucial to remember that anyone might experience the onset of OCD or any other mental health issue.

Environment, genetics, and family history
OCD runs in families. Simply said, if someone in your family carries it, there is a greater chance that a child will as well. Although no specific genes have yet been found to be connected to OCD, the familial pattern of OCD suggests that there may be a genetic component to the disorder.

It's crucial to remember that the environment matters when comparing nature and nurture. Over time, one can learn to develop obsessions and compulsions. Children may adopt these behavioral habits if they witness family members or other people dealing with OCD. Therefore, environmental exposures may contribute to the emergence of OCD.

Stressful Occasions
Stressful situations may put children with OCD at risk because they may already be vulnerable. Traumatized children may develop PTSD, which is sometimes mistaken for OCD.

Though OCD and PTSD both frequently involve unwelcome and intrusive thoughts that can resemble intrusive thoughts based on past traumatic events, OCD typically concentrates on uncertainty in the future and makes efforts to reduce them.

There is hope for treating and maintaining OCD!
It's crucial to remember that OCD cannot be cured. However, there are numerous approaches to managing this illness successfully.

There are extremely successful strategies to control obsessions and compulsions, even though persons with OCD will always have to live with some symptoms. Even if there are just minor symptoms that need to be controlled regularly, treatment can result in improvements in quality of life. OCD may not have any influence on a person's quality of life in the long run or with good therapy.

It's crucial to take an all-encompassing strategy while treating a youngster who has OCD. The best opportunity for children to make a significant recovery is when all aspects of OCD are treated effectively.

Every child with OCD receives treatment using a variety of strategies. Every diagnosis of OCD will respond differently to various therapies, similar to how each child is unique, thus it may be necessary to customize therapy to each patient to see which ones are most effective.

Therapy
CBT, or cognitive behavior therapy, is a common abbreviation for this treatment approach. Patients can connect their habits and thoughts with the aid of this therapy and others like it.

Exposure and response prevention therapy are one of the most crucial elements of CBT. This kind of therapy involves progressively exposing kids to a feared object or preoccupation.

Teens converse in class
Young individuals who deal with OCD can enjoy full and healthy lives with the right care.
For instance, a young child who fears germs might come into contact with dirt. The child then gains the ability to control their urge to perform compulsive rituals under the supervision of mental health professional.

Everyone in the family is impacted by OCD, so parents and siblings must learn how to effectively support kids. It has been established that family-based modalities of therapy are particularly effective. For children who are unwilling to get treatment, there are also parent-led therapeutic options. The parent gains knowledge about how to teach their child coping mechanisms.

Even though it takes time, this kind of therapy has been demonstrated to significantly raise the quality of life for kids who have OCD.

Medications

Children who have OCD may benefit from taking certain psychiatric drugs to help them manage their obsessions and compulsions. A serotonin reuptake inhibitor (SRI), a particular form of antidepressant, may be beneficial to add to the child's care plan if behavioral treatment is challenging to acquire or only seems to be marginally effective.

Children who have been diagnosed with OCD may take some of the most popular antidepressants, including:

Clomipramine is used in children ten years of age and older under the name Anafranil.
Children eight years of age or older utilize fluvoxamine.
Children seven years of age or older can use Prozac (fluoxetine).
Sertraline, the active ingredient in Zoloft, is used in children older than six.
Parents should thoroughly discuss all options with doctors before considering taking any medicine to fully understand the risks and advantages of each drug.

All psychiatric drugs may cause negative effects. Parents should be aware of potential adverse effects, the likelihood that they will manifest, how to recognize them, and when to talk to their doctor about perhaps stopping the medication.

Many youngsters who have been prescribed medication for OCD may be able to stop taking it once they have mastered and routinely practiced exposure and reaction prevention skills.

Providers and parents alike should consider each OCD experience as unique because it is. Once-weekly outpatient appointments are insufficient for some young people and their families. If that's the case, it might be beneficial to think about consulting a psychiatrist about medication.

A higher level of therapy, such as intensive outpatient or inpatient treatment, or a parent-only strategy to assist through family are further alternatives.

What Can I Do If I Think My Child Has OCD?

There is no shame in asking for aid for a child, so parents, guardians, and family members need to be aware of this. Additionally, children and teenagers need to understand that asking for help when they're having problems is completely acceptable and natural.

It's crucial to remember that kids with OCD are not irreparably hurt, broken, or damaged. It is simpler for children with OCD to open up about their issues when they are treated with compassion and understanding.

The first thing to do if you believe someone you know may be experiencing OCD is to not become alarmed. Even though the disorder may seem paralyzing, there are many ways to get the help your child needs. Child and their family can feel powerful and in charge of their mental health by seeking help and receiving treatment.

The child's care team should be informed of any potential OCD diagnoses to decide the best course of action. To get the help you require, contact your primary care physician or a nearby mental health center like McLean.

How Does Someone Get Formally Diagnosed With OCD?
The accurate diagnosis of a child requires several processes. A skilled practitioner, such as a psychiatrist or psychologist, will typically make this diagnosis with the help of other medical professionals, such as a pediatrician.

How to Prepare
Self-reporting and parent-reporting questionnaires, as well as in-person interviews, may be used in an examination to establish a diagnosis. To determine the presence of obsessions and rituals, these interviews involve particular questions.

A child is interviewed by a qualified expert about their emotions, thoughts, physical symptoms, and behavioral habits. Finding any specific obsessions or compulsions is the aim.

Then, a psychological assessment is conducted to determine the cause of these obsessions and compulsions. If things are not done in a certain manner, there must be anxiety or fear of a bad or "wrong" experience that might occur.

Lastly, it's critical to assess whether these actions negatively impact the child's quality of life. The evaluator frequently converses with the subject's friends and relatives throughout this evaluation.

The Diagnostic and Statistical Manual of Mental Health Disorders, commonly abbreviated as DSM-5, contains criteria that the psychiatrist utilizes to make the formal diagnosis. This serves as a manual for mental health professionals and was issued by the American Psychiatric Association.

It's crucial to rule out alternative causes of this behavior before making an OCD diagnosis. Consequently, a physical examination might be conducted to look for symptoms and issues that could be connected to OCD complications or a potential alternate diagnosis.
Obsessive-compulsive disorder is one of the most prevalent mental health disorders. Despite this, there are widespread myths about how OCD manifests in people that can make it difficult for many to comprehend the condition.

OCD cases are all as individual as the people who are diagnosed with it, and there are numerous myths surrounding the condition. Several myths about OCD have surfaced, and many people now loosely refer to perfectionism as "being OCD."

Through research and training, we can: broaden access to quality care; promote a positive and encouraging environment for people with OCD and the medical professionals who care for them; and combat the stigma associated with mental illness.

OCD Massachusetts, a non-profit affiliate of the IOCDF, seeks to educate the public and professionals about OCD to increase awareness and enhance the standard of care offered in Massachusetts. Additionally, they promote and lobby for the Massachusetts OCD community while working to increase the availability of resources for people with OCD and their families.
.Even by itself, obsessive-compulsive disorder (OCD) presents difficulties. But how do you raise kids whose brains seem to be continuously on the lookout for danger? What should you do when you have to take care of a youngster yet a distracting notion won't leave your mind?

Some kids have what they could refer to as "children OCD," where they constantly fear that something has happened to them and stress over little things. If you don't have OCD, it's difficult to explain, but imagine your typical parental anxiety dialed up to extreme levels.

Other times, a child's compulsions and obsessions have little to do with the care they receive from their parents, yet they nonetheless have an impact on family life. After supper, Dad can't enter the kitchen because he'll begin obsessively cleaning it. Mom is terrified she'll run into the middle of a busy roadway if she leaves the house with the infant.

These difficulties surely ring all too true if you have OCD. You might even think that having OCD makes it impossible to be a good parent. It's simple to comprehend this presumption.

Additionally, it is wholly incorrect.

Though it may not always be as simple as deciding to be better, you can surely be there for your children in the way you want to. It entails taking charge of your OCD and identifying the best medication to treat your symptoms. Although it requires work, as you are aware, your family is worth the effort. For parents who are coping with OCD
Myth: Those who have OCD desire perfection in all things.
People with OCD may engage in perfectionism-related behaviors or obsess about flawless things. However, they usually result from efforts to lessen anxiety or distress brought on by uncertainty or a certain consequence that is dreaded, not from a desire for perfection
.

Chapter 2

How to handle ocd

Does your kid possess:
persistent, unsettling anxieties, trepidations, or worries?
absurd, routine religeous practices?
unwanted, uncontrollable th100Typically, OCD runs in families. Thus, it might be genetic. However, it can also happen if there is no family history of OCD. Streptococcal infections can sometimes cause OCD or exacerbate it.

What signs of OCD do children show?
Each youngster may exhibit a unique set of symptoms. The most typical signs are as follows:

intense preoccupation with dirt or pathogens
persistent uncertainties, such as whether the door is locked
conflicting ideas about using violence, causing injury to or killing someone, or harming oneself
Counting, touching, and thinking about numbers and sequences for extended periods of time
obsession with precision, symmetry, or order
persistent thoughts of engaging in inappropriate or banned behaviors
having doubts about one's personal religious convictions
a strong desire to remember or be aware of even the smallest details
Too much focus on details

excessive fear of the worst happening aggressive thoughts, desires, or actions

You observe a friend neatly packing away their work tools as you are both working on a project. You can't help but notice that they've arranged all of their pens in their box so that they are facing the same way and are arranged in order of color. They reply, "Oh." That's just me being OCD,

OCD is frequently so much more than the disorder that is frequently associated with neatness and particularity.

OCD can have a particularly negative impact on children. Any period, possibly as early as three years old, can see the start of symptoms.

To ensure that kids and teenagers who are at risk of developing OCD receive the proper care, parents and teachers must be aware of the risk factors.

OCD is treatable when properly managed. Neglecting it could have major consequences for the child's and the family members' quality of life.
HowContinue to Read to Discover
ROLE OF PARENTS IN MANAGING OCD
How to spot signs of OCD in children and teenagers
How to effectively manage and treat OCD in children
OCD: What Is It?
A pattern of unwanted and bothersome thoughts, concerns, pictures, or sensations that cause distress (such as anxiety, disgust, or "not right" sensations) and repetitive behaviors intended to soothe that distress are the hallmarks of obsessive compulsive disorder.

These undesirable thoughts are frequently referred to as obsessions. Compulsions are unwanted, recurrent habits or mental practices.

Most people occasionally have unwelcome thoughts throughout their lives. These undesirable ideas won't be taken seriously if the person does not have OCD, thus they won't be as distressing. Obsessions and compulsions that have a clinically negative effect on a child's life are the distinguishing feature of OCD.

For instance, unpleasant thoughts may be so severe that kids have problems falling asleep at night. The child may have trouble leaving the house to go to school, play sports, or carry out their daily routine because the repetitive behaviors are so upsetting and hindering.

a doctor converses with a young girl
For a child or teen, OCD can be devastating, but with the right psychiatric care, there is hope.

The good news is that OCD has been extensively researched and that there are effective treatments available. Similar to other mental health disorders, this condition can be treated more quickly the earlier it is diagnosed.

It is critical to examine the obsessions and compulsions that underlie OCD in detail in order to provide children with the care they require.

What Are Obsessions, Exactly?
Concerning OCD, obsessions are fears that kids, teens, and other people can't stop thinking about. OCD sufferers frequently recognize that something is "wrong," and they frequently realize that the thoughts they are having are abnormal.

Despite their best attempts, people appear unable to stop thinking about these things, which might make them anxious.

The following are a few of the most typical types of obsessions:

fear that no matter what they do, they will pass away or become ill
Fear that a loved one will suffer harm, become ill, or pass away Worry that they will break a law and receive a harsh punishment for it
Fear of touching things out of concern that they might be dirty
Obsession with making sure that everything is organized, even, and in its proper place
Fear that if something isn't done in a certain order, bad things will happen.
The fact is that everyone occasionally has unwanted thoughts. The distinction between OCD and sporadic unwanted thoughts is that children with OCD can't stop thinking about these thoughts and sometimes become paralyzed by them. These obsessions are frequently so severe that children are unable to think about anything else.

What Are Compulsions, Exactly?
A youngster must experience both obsessions and compulsions in order to be diagnosed with OCD.

Compulsions are strict and frequently repeating mental or behavioral patterns. These compulsive behaviors, which frequently take the shape of routines, are intended to reduce stress or avert potentially terrifying results.

Children with OCD must repeat these acts in a specific sequence over and over again. If they don't, their obsessions take control and they start to worry that something bad will happen. These actions could be related to symmetry, cleanliness, orderliness, or safety. Children are forced to start over if they aren't done "exactly right."

These actions might be thought of as rituals that provide kids a source of power. They believe they can influence what happens next by performing these repeating behaviors in a specific way.

The following are some of the most prevalent examples of compulsions:

having to consistently wash or clean items a certain way
Repeating phrases in your head until they "feel correct"
having to repeatedly recreate, edit, or read something after erasing it
To say a word or phrase more times than necessary until it is uttered precisely once or in precisely the proper way
ensuring that every door in the house is locked several times, or repeatedly going in and out of the doors
checking to make sure all of the lights are out before you leave the house
ensuring that each homework assignment was completed correctly by reviewing it a predetermined number of times.
chewing each bite the same amount of times on both sides of the mouth
arranging everything in a predetermined, even, symmetrical arrangement
counting everything and anything to specific lucky numbers to avoid bad numbers
It's crucial to remember that compulsions frequently develop from adaptive habits. Children should, for instance, double-check their homework to make sure it was completed correctly.

On the other hand, this starts to have a clinically negative effect on not just their life but also the lives of family members if kids wind up checking their homework a dozen times to the disadvantage of other activities.

The same may be said for making sure that doors are closed and that all lights are off. Before departing, it's a good idea to check sure the residence is secure. However, this becomes a significant problem if it stops the family from leaving the house.

Taking Back Her Freedom
Patient and doctor
Learn about the struggle a young patient faced to beat OCD.

Controlling Her OCD
How Can OCD in Children Be Spotted?
Recognizing the potential symptoms of OCD in children is crucial for people like parents, teachers, and athletic coaches. The sooner you can step in at the first sign of a mental health issue, the greater the likelihood that the intervention will be beneficial.

There are many typical developmental rituals, such as sleep rituals, that are not related to OCD. But if a ritual starts to interfere with a child's ability to function, that can help determine whether it's more than just a routine and may be an indication of OCD.

OCD frequently grows gradually over time. Due to the gradual onset of symptoms and a parent's innate desire to comfort and protect their child, it may be challenging for adults to recognize a child's OCD symptoms when they first emerge.

It might be simpler to see how OCD affects children's and people around them's quality of life.

There are a number of things to look out for that could be OCD symptoms.

Not all of the following symptoms indicate OCD. They are illustrations of actions that might indicate that a young person is in distress and may require assistance from a qualified adult.

Homework
OCD in children can cause them to take too long to finish their assignments. Children may be required to read the same passage repeatedly, write each number exactly as they appear in a math problem, or have their schoolwork checked so many times that it takes a very long time to complete.

Away from the House
When leaving the house, a family with OCD-affected children may take longer.

For instance, if a youngster is spending a long time to get dressed, they may be making sure that every door, window, and light are in the "correct" places or working properly before leaving. They could become upset if they try to leave before the ritual is done.

The family is frequently perpetually late for activities as a result of this tendency.

Handwashing
When it comes to OCD, handwashing is one of the most well-known compulsions.

Handwashing may be motivated by obsessions with germs, feelings of disgust or other types of contamination, such as "bad emotions," or worries about becoming stressed, anxious, or worried all the time. Look for any evidence of raw, bleeding skin on the hands if handwashing is associated with OCD.

If kids wash their hands frequently during the day, the soap will irritate their skin, causing scarring, skin peeling, and bleeding.

Alcohol or drugs

Children may use drugs as a coping method occasionally when they are having trouble managing a condition. Teens who are struggling with their mental health may feel overwhelmed, misunderstood, or socially isolated. On sometimes, this results in drug abuse.

Sleep Patterns

OCD frequently interferes with getting to sleep or staying asleep. OCD children might need to follow a very specific regimen before going to bed and drifting off to sleep. If individuals experience intrusive thoughts or worries that are more acute at night, they can also have trouble falling asleep. They have to start the process afresh if it is interrupted for any reason.

OCD frequently extends the bedtime routine by 30 minutes, an hour, or even more. Children are deprived of essential sleep, which affects their ability to learn, their emotional growth, and their interactions with peers and family members.

Consistent sleep disruption can also have a detrimental impact on how well CBT and other OCD therapies work.

Don't forget

Not all of the manifestations of OCD in children are represented by these behaviors. Additionally, it does not imply that if a child has problems with them, they have OCD.

These are just a few instances where a young child could have uncomfortable thoughts, feelings, or sensations and then act out or avoid the situation to feel better.

Parents should think considering talking to a qualified expert about the possibility of OCD if this cycle of discomfort and relief causes family distress or dysfunction.

View Now!

Obsessive compulsive disorder is highlighted by Dr. Elizabeth McIngvale.

Like other mental health conditions, there is seldom just one cause for a child to acquire OCD.

The following list of risk factors is far from exhaustive, but it does give a brief overview of what might contribute to the emergence of OCD. It is crucial to remember that anyone might experience the onset of OCD or any other mental health issue.

Environment, genetics, and family history

OCD runs in families. Simply said, if someone in your family carries it, there is a greater chance that a child will as well. Although no specific genes have yet been found to be connected to OCD, the familial pattern of OCD suggests that there may be a genetic component to the disorder.

It's crucial to remember that the environment matters when comparing nature and nurture. Over time, one can learn to develop obsessions and compulsions. Children may adopt these behavioral habits if they witness family members or other people dealing with OCD. Therefore, environmental exposures may contribute to the emergence of OCD.

Stressful Occasions

Stressful situations may put children with OCD at risk because they may already be vulnerable. Traumatized children may develop PTSD, which is sometimes mistaken for OCD.

Though OCD and PTSD both frequently involve unwelcome and intrusive thoughts that can resemble intrusive thoughts based on past traumatic events, OCD typically concentrates on uncertainty in the future and makes efforts to reduce them.

There is hope for treating and maintaining OCD!

It's crucial to remember that OCD cannot be cured. However, there are numerous approaches to managing this illness successfully.

There are extremely successful strategies to control obsessions and compulsions, even though persons with OCD will always have to live with some symptoms. Even if there are just minor symptoms that need to be controlled on a regular basis, treatment can result in improvements in quality of life. OCD may not have any influence on a person's quality of life in the long run or with good therapy.

It's crucial to take an all-encompassing strategy while treating a youngster who has OCD. The best opportunity for children to make a significant recovery is when all aspects of OCD are treated effectively.

Every child with OCD receives treatment using a variety of strategies. Every diagnosis of OCD will respond differently to various therapies, similar to how each child is unique, thus it may be necessary to customize therapy to each patient to see which ones are most effective.

Therapy

CBT, or cognitive behavior therapy, is a common abbreviation for this treatment approach. Patients can connect their habits and thoughts with the aid of this therapy and others like it.

Exposure and response prevention therapy is one of the most crucial elements of CBT. This kind of therapy involves progressively exposing kids to a feared object or preoccupation.

Teens converse in class

Young individuals who deal with OCD can enjoy full and healthy lives with the right care.

For instance, a young child who fears germs might come into contact with dirt. The child then gains the ability to control their urge to perform compulsive rituals under the supervision of a mental health professional.

Everyone in the family is impacted by OCD, so parents and siblings must learn how to effectively support kids. It has been established that family-based modalities of therapy are particularly effective. For children who are unwilling to get treatment, there are also parent-led therapeutic options. The parent gains knowledge about how to teach their child coping mechanisms.

Even though it takes time, this kind of therapy has been demonstrated to significantly raise the quality of life for kids who have OCD.

Medications

Children who have OCD may benefit from taking certain psychiatric drugs to help them manage their obsessions and compulsions. A serotonin reuptake inhibitor (SRI), a particular form of antidepressant, may be beneficial to add to the child's care plan if behavioral treatment is challenging to acquire or only seems to be marginally effective.

Children who have been diagnosed with OCD may take some of the most popular antidepressants, including:

Clomipramine is used in children ten years of age and older under the name Anafranil.

Children eight years of age or older utilize fluvoxamine.

Children seven years of age or older can use Prozac (fluoxetine).

Sertraline, the active ingredient in Zoloft, is used in children older than six.

Parents should thoroughly discuss all options with doctors before considering taking any medicine in order to fully understand the risks and advantages of each drug.

All psychiatric drugs may cause negative effects. Parents should be aware of potential adverse effects, the likelihood that they will manifest, how to recognize them, and when to talk to their doctor about perhaps stopping medication.

Many youngsters who are prescribed medication for OCD may be able to stop taking it once they have mastered and routinely practiced exposure and reaction prevention skills.

Providers and parents alike should consider each OCD experience as unique because it is. Once-weekly outpatient appointments are insufficient for some young people and their families. If that's the case, it might be beneficial to think about consulting a psychiatrist about medication.

A higher level of therapy, such as intense outpatient or inpatient treatment, or a parent-only strategy to assist through family are further alternatives.

What Can I Do If I Think My Child Has OCD?

There is no shame in asking for aid for a child, so parents, guardians, and family members need to be aware of this. Additionally, children and teenagers need to understand that asking for help when they're having problems is completely acceptable and natural.

It's crucial to remember that kids with OCD are not irreparably hurt, broken, or damaged. It is simpler for children with OCD to open up about their issues when they are treated with compassion and understanding.

The first thing to do if you believe someone you know may be experiencing OCD is to not become alarmed. Despite the fact that the disorder may seem paralyzing, there are many ways to get the help your child needs. A child and their family can feel powerful and in charge of their mental health by seeking help and receiving treatment.

The child's care team should be informed of any potential OCD diagnoses in order to decide the best course of action. To get the help you require, contact your primary care physician or a nearby mental health center like McLean.

How Does Someone Get Formally Diagnosed With OCD?

The accurate diagnosis of a child requires several processes. A skilled practitioner, such as a psychiatrist or psychologist, will typically make this diagnosis with the help of other medical professionals, such as a pediatrician.

How to Prepare

Self-reporting and parent-reporting questionnaires, as well as in-person interviews, may be used in an examination to establish a diagnosis. To determine the presence of obsessions and rituals, these interviews involve particular questions.

A child is interviewed by a qualified expert about their emotions, thoughts, physical symptoms, and behavioral habits. Finding any specific obsessions or compulsions is the aim.

Then, a psychological assessment is conducted in an effort to determine the cause of these obsessions and compulsions. If things are not done a certain manner, there must be anxiety or fear of a bad or "wrong" experience that might occur.

Lastly, it's critical to assess whether these actions negatively impact the child's quality of life. The evaluator frequently converses with the subject's friends and relatives throughout this evaluation.

The Diagnostic and Statistical Manual of Mental Health Disorders, commonly abbreviated as DSM-5, contains criteria that the psychiatrist utilizes to make the formal diagnosis. This serves as a manual for mental health professionals and was issued by the American Psychiatric Association.

It's crucial to rule out alternative causes of this behavior before making an OCD diagnosis. Consequently, a physical examination might be conducted to look for symptoms and issues that could be connected to OCD complications or a potential alternate diagnosis.
Obsessive compulsive disorder is one of the most prevalent mental health disorders. Despite this, there are widespread myths about how OCD manifests in people that can make it difficult for many to comprehend the condition.

OCD cases are all as individual as the people who are diagnosed with it, and there are numerous myths surrounding the condition. Several myths about OCD have surfaced, and many people now loosely refer to perfectionism as "being OCD."

Through research and training, we can: broaden access to quality care; promote a positive and encouraging environment for people with OCD and the medical professionals who care for them; and combat the stigma associated with mental illness.

OCD Massachusetts, a non-profit affiliate of the IOCDF, seeks to educate the public and professionals about OCD in order to increase awareness and enhance the standard of care offered in Massachusetts. Additionally, they promote and lobby for the

Massachusetts OCD community while working to increase the availability of resources for people with OCD and their families.
.Even by itself, obsessive-compulsive disorder (OCD) presents difficulties. But how do you raise kids whose brains seem to be continuously on the lookout for danger? What should you do when you have to take care of a youngster yet a distracting notion won't leave your mind?

Some kids have what they could refer to as "children OCD," where they constantly fear that something has happened to them and stress over little things. If you don't have OCD, it's difficult to explain, but imagine your typical parental anxiety dialed up to extreme levels.

Other times, a child's compulsions and obsessions have little to do with the care they receive from their parents, yet they nonetheless have an impact on family life. After supper, Dad can't enter the kitchen because he'll begin obsessively cleaning it. Mom is terrified she'll run into the middle of a busy roadway if she leaves the house with the infant.

These difficulties surely ring all too true if you have OCD. You might even think that having OCD makes it impossible to be a good parent. It's simple to comprehend this presumption.

Additionally, it is wholly incorrect.

Though it may not always be as simple as making the decision to be better, you can surely be there for your children in the way you want to. It entails taking charge of your OCD and identifying the best medication to treat your symptoms. Although it requires work, as you are aware, your family is worth the effort. For parents who are coping with OCD Myth: Those who have OCD desire perfection in all things.
People with OCD may engage in perfectionism-related behaviors or obsess about things that are flawless. However, they usually result from efforts to lessen anxiety or distress brought on by uncertainty or a certain consequence that is dreaded, not from a desire for perfection
psychiatrists, may provide care for your child. The care team for your child will be determined by their needs and how severe their OCD is.
Maintain constant, honest contact with your youngster. OCD sufferers in children may feel ashamed of their condition.
Inform people of your child's disorder. To develop a treatment plan, consult with your child's doctor, school, and other relevant parties.
Request assistance from the neighborhood community services. It may be beneficial to stay in touch with other parents whose children suffer from OCD.

Important facts concerning childhood OCD

One kind of anxiety illness is OCD. Unwanted obsessive thoughts plague a child with OCD. They are connected to anxieties, like interacting with filthy stuff. To manage their worries, the toddler engages in compulsive behaviors like washing their hands. The person doing the rituals may feel either rational or irrational while doing so. The youngster could not comprehend the significance of these rituals. They can feel ashamed of the uncontrollable behaviors that they exhibit.

OCD's precise root cause is uncertain. Serotonin, a brain neurotransmitter, is deficient in OCD sufferers' brains.

Recurrent doubts and a severe fixation with filth or germs are examples of obsessional symptoms.

Constant checking and object hoarding are examples of compulsive behaviour.

To diagnose OCD, a mental health evaluation is required.

Therapy and medication are all part of treatment.

Next actions

Following are some pointers to help you make the most of a visit to your child's doctor:

Understand your objectives for the visit and the reason you are there.

Make a list of the questions you want answered before your visit.

Write down any new diagnoses, medications, treatments, or tests that were performed at the appointment. Any new advice your provider gives you for your child should also be noted.

Understand the benefits of any new medications or treatments prescribed for your child. Also be aware of any potential negative effects.

See if there are any other options for treating your child's condition.

Understand the potential meaning of the results from a test or operation before undergoing it.

Understand what to expect if your child refuses the medication, test, or operation.

Note the date, time, and reason for any follow-up appointments your kid may have.

Learn how to reach the provider of your child's care after business hours. This is crucial if your child gets sick and you have inquiries or require guidance.

Chapter 3

Medications for ocd

key supportive role in your child's treatment. Here are things you can do to help your child:

Keep all appointments with your child's healthcare provider.

Talk with your child's healthcare provider about other providers who will be included in your child's care. Your child may get care from a team that may include counselors, therapists, social workers, psychologists, and psychiatrists. Your child's care team will depend on your child's needs and how serious the OCD is.

Keep strong and open lines of communication with your child. Children with OCD can feel embarrassed about their disorder.

Tell others about your child's disorder. Work with your child's healthcare provider and school to create a treatment plan.

Reach out for support from local community services. Being in touch with other parents who have a child with OCD may be helpful.

Key points about OCD in children

OCD is a type of anxiety disorder. A child with OCD has obsessive thoughts that are not wanted. They are linked to fears, such as touching dirty objects. The child uses compulsive rituals such as handwashing to control the fears. These rituals may feel rational or irrational to the person doing them. The child may not understand why they do these rituals. They may feel embarrassed that the behaviors occur and can't be controlled.

The exact cause of OCD is unknown. Children with OCD don't have enough of a chemical called serotonin in their brain.

Obsessive symptoms include repeated doubts and extreme preoccupation with dirt or germs.

Compulsive behaviors include hoarding objects and checking things often.

A mental health evaluation is needed to diagnose OCD.

Treatment includes therapy and medicine.

Next steps

Tips to help you get the most from a visit to your child's healthcare provider:

Know the reason for the visit and what you want to happen.

Before your visit, write down questions you want answered.

At the visit, write down the name of a new diagnosis, and any new medicines, treatments, or tests. Also write down any new instructions your provider gives you for your child.

Know why a new medicine or treatment is prescribed and how it will help your child. Also know what the side effects are.

Ask if your child's condition can be treated in other ways.

Know why a test or procedure is recommended and what the results could mean.

Know what to expect if your child does not take the medicine or have the test or procedure.

If your child has a follow-up appointment, write down the date, time, and purpose for that visit.

Know how you can contact your child's provider after office hours. This is important if your child becomes ill and you have questions or need advice

Chapter 4

Things parents get wrong about OCD

The most misunderstood issue in my therapy practice is childhood OCD. I have lost count of how many parents I have talked to who completely misinterpret their children's OCD behaviors.

These are caring, well intentioned parents. Parents who have been bombarded with media images of stereotypical, one dimensional characters who distort and simplify OCD.

Parents often have incorrect assumptions about Childhood OCD. Don't be one of them!

We can also blame OCD itself for being the master of disguises. OCD can manifest in a large amount of unique ways – all of which look completely different from one another.

It is not surprising then that parents often miss the mark completely when it comes to childhood OCD. Parents have many distorted beliefs about OCD, but there are a few that are consistent among most of them.

You have to be clean, neat and organized to have OCD

Often when I tell parents their child is exhibiting OCD symptoms, I will get a look of bafflement and comments such as, "Oh no. He definitely does not have OCD. If you saw his room you wouldn't say that!"

I wholeheartedly blame the media for this one. Not everyone who has OCD is a neat freak. In fact, most are not.

OCD is about obsessive thoughts and compulsive actions. These obsessive thoughts can be an array of themes – most of which have nothing to do with cleanliness.

Kids with childhood OCD might constantly have to tap or touch things. They might have to count their steps. They might have to confess behaviors they have never done. For a comprehensive list of obsessive thoughts and compulsive actions click here. You'll see the list is long.

Kids do rituals for attention

Out of all the misperceptions one can have about OCD – this one saddens me the most. Parents will sometimes argue with me that their children are doing rituals for attention. I will hear comments like, "He just wants our attention, so we punish him" or "We ignore her because we know she is just trying to bother us."

These perceptions couldn't be farther from the truth. Children with OCD are tormented by their ritualistic behavior. If anything, they are more likely to try and conceal their behavior than draw attention to it.

OCD rituals are just tics, quirky behavior or habits

Sometimes when I am getting background history from parents they will mention things like, "He has these quirky habits he does sometimes. We just ignore them and they usually go away, but something pops up in its place." When I explore further – they will often proceed to describe an OCD ritual.

It is understandable that some OCD rituals can be misinterpreted as tics or strange habits. If you don't know what to look for, these behaviors can look very similar.

I have worked with kids that have to move their eyes in a certain pattern, that have to touch their hands to their heart, that have to blow air out of their mouths or have to clear their throats after certain thoughts. All of these behaviors can be easily misinterpreted.

OCD is a phase children will grow out of eventually

The most dangerous assumption is that OCD is just a phase. Parents shouldn't take a wait and see approach with OCD. Childhood OCD doesn't typically just fade into the sunset.

No, it makes itself cozy in your children's head constantly creating more rules and more rituals. The longer parents wait to get treatment, the harder it will be to help their children overcome their OCD.

If you suspect your children might be exhibiting signs of childhood OCD, have them evaluated by a mental health professional. It is better to be proactive than reactive when it comes to childhood OCD. An evaluation can't hurt, but holding on to these false assumptions can.

Know someone who has some of these misperceptions? Share this book with them.

SOME FREQUENTLY ASKED QUESTIONS:
My child's obsessions are severe, and it would be traumatic for her not to do her compulsions. Would ERP be painful and difficult for her?
Your child's therapist will ask your child to rank her obsessions and compulsions in order from the mildest to the most severe. Starting slowly with the easiest symptoms, the therapist will design small challenges that will teach your child to delay

compulsions briefly, then for increasingly longer periods of time.
ERP is hard work, and it can be difficult for parents to see their children struggle to reach a goal. But the rewards and benefits of successful ERP are enormous.
Living with untreated OCD is vastly more painful than any discomfort associated with ERP. Early intervention helps prevent your child from missing out on important developmental milestones and activities.
Untreated OCD can worsen as a child gets older. Some adults with OCD have such severe symptoms that they are unable to work or live on their own. Committing to treatment as a top priority can give your son or daughter skills to manage the disorder for life.
I work fulltime and my son is in school, but it's hard to schedule ERP appointments in the evenings or on weekends. Do we have to miss school and work for treatment?
Parents often need to miss work to get medical care for a child. Your employer's human resources department might be able to help you schedule absences for appointments.
Untreated OCD can interfere significantly with a child's education, so it makes sense for him to miss school from time to time for his therapy appointments. ERP therapy will give him the skills he needs to manage his symptoms at school and at home

Even though movies and television shows sometimes treat OCD as a joke, it's very serious to the people who have to live with it every day and to their family members. Once considered a rare disorder, doctors have learned that OCD affects millions of people around the world.
Approximately five million to six million Americans have OCD that's between 2 percent and 3 percent of the population.
If OCD affects only two other family members, that means some 21 million people in the United States are touched by the disorder.
OCD strikes about one in 50 adults and about one in 100 schoolaged children.
OCD is the fourth most common psychiatric diagnosis, after phobias, substance abuse and major depression.
OCD ranks among the 10 leading causes of disability worldwide, according to one international study.

Support
Other parents whose children have completed treatment can be a valuable source of information and support. Meeting other kids with OCD can make a world of difference to your child by helping him or her realize that the disorder is common and treatable. Support groups and self-help groups may be available in your area. The Internet also has groups, message boards, and web sites devoted to OCD. Caution is necessary when using the web, as not every idea or treatment found online will be safe, effective, or

scientifically tested.

Is ERP expensive?
Like many of the things we do to help our kids succeed in the world — for example, braces and prescription eyeglasses — ERP therapy requires a financial commitment as well as our time. But the benefit of ERP therapy to a child with OCD can be priceless; it can give your child the skills to manage the disorder for life. Ask your child's therapist about fees, and check with your health insurance plan to see if therapy is a covered benefit.
What about alternative and natural remedies?
No alternative remedies have been proven effective for OCD. It is important to check with your child's doctor before using herbal supplements, since some herbs can interfere with prescription medications.
My daughter has been seeing a therapist whom she really likes, but her therapist is not a cognitive behavior therapist and does not practice ERP. Should we change to a new treatment provider?
ERP is the only therapy that can reduce the symptoms of OCD. If your daughter benefits from her current therapist in other ways she may wish to continue these visits. But to reduce OCD symptoms, she will need ERP.
Why can't we just use medicine to treat our child's OCD?
ERP therapy is the treatment of choice for Obsessive Compulsive Disorder and should be tried before medication is considered. It is possible that your child can manage OCD with therapy alone. Medication can partially relieve symptoms, but it cannot teach your child to manage the disorder. For some children, a combination of ERP therapy and medication is the most effective treatment. Some children require medication for a short time to ease OCD symptoms enough for them to succeed in ERP therapy.

Exposure and Response
Prevention Therapy
to find a
ERP, which is a form of cognitive behavior therapy, is the only form of psychotherapy proven effective in treating Obsessive Compulsive Disorder. It is recommended by nationally recognized institutions such as the National Institutes of Mental Health, Mayo Clinic, and Harvard Medical School. Some studies show that more than 80 percent of the people who complete a course of ERP therapy experience a significant reduction in OCD symptoms.
Exposure and response prevention puts participants in situations that

expose them to their obsessions and simultaneously prevents them from performing the compulsions they use to ease the accompanying anxiety. Although ERP therapy deliberately induces anxiety, it does so in a controlled and gradual way for the purpose of getting better.

For example, a child with contamination obsessions might be asked to touch a doorknob — this act is called an "exposure" because it exposes her to her fear of germs and creates anxiety. The response prevention part of the therapy then keeps her from washing her

mental health professional who has experience in treating children using ERP therapy.

hands, which is the compulsion she feels driven to perform to ease the anxiety.

Preparing for ERP

After scheduling an appointment with an experienced cognitive behavior therapist, prepare for your visit by taking notes about your child's behavior and your questions and concerns. Familiarize yourself with OCD by referring to the materials listed at the end of this publication. You can also help prepare your child for treatment by using the books listed for children of various ages.

ERP is not traditional "talk therapy." It works by using exercises and other active techniques that teach the child to respond differently to obsessive urges and thought patterns.

OCD does not respond to forms of therapy that explore issues of self-esteem, peer pressure, family dynamics, or early childhood junctures such as toilet training in the belief that working on these issues will help a child's OCD. Although talk therapy is not an effective treatment for OCD, it can be helpful for other matters, such as family issues and peer relationship problems.

Most children in ERP therapy meet with their therapist once a week, although more frequent meetings may be appropriate in severe cases that require intensive treatment. A typical course of ERP takes 10 to 15 weeks. Changes in your child's symptoms may not be apparent for several weeks, and significant changes can take 10 weeks to occur. If no significant change is apparent after 10 or 15 weeks, discuss the treatment plan with your

child's therapist.
An inpatient treatment center may be an option in extremely severe cases or when no outpatient ERP is available.

OCD and the Family:
When a child has Obsessive Compulsive Disorder, the symptoms can impact the entire family and present parenting challenges for which most moms and dads are unprepared. Siblings may feel confused, guilty, sympathetic, and resentful all at once.
Parents often experience feelings of frustration, guilt, and dismay as their child's obsessions and compulsions fail to respond to reason, common sense, or traditional parenting skills.
Your child's therapist can work separately with you and your family to teach you how to respond to your child's symptoms in a helpful way.
The therapist will teach family members to disentangle themselves gradually from the child's OCD, especially if they have been helping with compulsions and rituals. Accommodating symptoms strengthens the disorder, not your child. Successful treatment may require you to rethink the way you respond to OCD.
The parent is a crucial member of a child's ERP therapy team. The therapist will help you
understand how to:
recognize OCD behaviors
talk to your child about OCD
help your child by gradually changing your response
to his or her obsessions and compulsions
model behavior goals for your child
Accommodating
symptoms
strengthens
the disorder,
not your child.
support your child, not the OCD

OCD at School:

Obtaining appropriate treatment for your child's OCD can be essential for success in the classroom. Left untreated, OCD can have a devastating impact on a child's education.

Time-consuming rituals can interfere with homework and sleep. Obsessions and compulsions can increase absenteeism and tardiness. A child distracted by obsessive fears often appears inattentive. Symptoms that occur at school can result in incomplete homework and social problems. Some kids with OCD are isolated or teased. Most children with the disorder have average to above-average IQs, but many struggle to succeed in school because of their symptoms.

If symptoms are interfering with your child's education, then an educational intervention should be part of your child's treatment. Providing the school with information about the disorder can help teachers understand your child's needs so they can support your child and make any necessary adjustments. An ERP therapist can help you decide how to tell your child's teachers about OCD. Educators who understand the disorder can help build your child's social skills and self-esteem and restore his or her dignity and confidence in the classroom.

Educational consultants who specialize in accommodations for OCD and related disorders can help parents work with schools so that their child can succeed academically while learning to manage the disorder in the classroom. It is your right under the Individuals with Disabilities Education Act (IDEA) to request appropriate modifications in your child's educational environment related to OCD symptoms. These accommodations may only need to be temporary while your child is learning to manage his or her OCD.

www.ingramcontent.com/pod-product-compliance
Lightning Source LLC
LaVergne TN
LVHW020535160826
845677LV00015B/4080
* 9 7 9 8 3 5 8 9 5 7 9 8 5 *